WITHDRAWN

Master
the Library
and
Media Center

Ann Graham Gaines

Enslow Elementary

an imprint of

 Enslow Publishers, Inc.

40 Industrial Road
Box 398
Berkeley Heights, NJ 07922
USA

http://www.enslow.com

Enslow Elementary, an imprint of Enslow Publishers, Inc.

Enslow Elementary® is a registered trademark of Enslow Publishers, Inc.

Library of Congress Cataloging-in-Publication Data
Gaines, Ann.
  Master the library and media center / Ann Graham Gaines.
     p. cm. — (Ace it! information literacy series)
  Includes bibliographical references and index.
  Summary: "Readers will learn about both the regular and electronic research materials
available at the library"—Provided by publisher.
  ISBN-13: 978-0-7660-3393-1
  ISBN-10: 0-7660-3393-7
  1. Library research—Juvenile literature. 2. Research—Methodology—Juvenile literature.
3. Information resources—Juvenile literature. 4. Information literacy—Juvenile literature.
5. Libraries—Juvenile literature. 6. Instructional materials center—Juvenile literature. I.
Title.
  Z710.G23 2009
  020.72—dc22

                              2008024886

Printed in the United States of America
112009 Lake Book Manufacturing, Inc., Melrose Park, IL

10 9 8 7 6 5 4 3 2

To Our Readers:
We have done our best to make sure all Internet Addresses in this book were active and
appropriate when we went to press. However, the author and the publisher have no control
over and assume no liability for the material available on those Internet sites or on other
Web sites they may link to. Any comments or suggestions can be sent by e-mail to
comments@enslow.com or to the address on the back cover.

♻ Enslow Publishers, Inc., is committed to printing our books on recycled paper. The
paper in every book contains 10% to 30% post-consumer waste (PCW). The cover board on
the outside of each book contains 100% PCW. Our goal is to do our part to help young
people and the environment too!

Cover photo: iStockphoto.com/Jacek Chabraszewski; iStockphoto.com/Alex Nikada (background).
Interior photos: Corbis/Gabe Palmer, p. 4; Corbis/LWA-Sharie Kennedy, p. 22; The Image
Works/Jeff Greenberg, p. 10; The Image Works/Bob Daemmrich, p. 13; The Image Works/David
Lassman/Syracuse Newspapers, p. 14; iStockphoto.com/Andres Peiro, pp. 3, 5, 11, 23, 31, 39, 41;
iStockphoto.com/Lisa F. Young, p. 12 (center of web page); iStockphoto.com/Chris Schmidt, p. 12
(bottom of web page); iStockphoto.com/Aldo Murillo, pp. 12, 18, 19, (top of web page), 30, 40;
iStockphoto.com/Chris Dascher, p. 24; Courtesy of Glenn Magpuri, San Diego Miramar College
Library, p. 20; Mary Francis McGavic (illustrations), pp. 12, 15, 18, 19; Photo Edit/Bill Aron, p. 6;
Photo Edit/John Neubauer, p. 9; Photo Edit/ Spencer Grant, p. 17; Photo Edit/Jonathan Nourok, p.
28; Photo Edit/Mary Kate Denny, p. 34; Photo Edit/ Bill Aron, p. 37; Photolibrary.com/Thomas
Barwick, p. 38.

Contents

A library is a welcoming place to work—and to have fun!

1

Off to the Library!

If you go to a public library, you will find that it is packed with people. Many of them are kids like you. What are they doing there? Kids go to the library for many different reasons. One is just to have fun! At the library you can pick out a book to read, flip through the latest magazines, check out a new DVD, or listen to music.

Kids also go to the library to do research. When you do research, you hunt for information about something that interests you. You search through sources, like books, magazines, and newspapers, to find information and to answer your questions.

Kids often do research for a school assignment. You might also do research as part of an after-school activity. For example, you might enter a science fair, or you want to earn a scout badge. Then you will have to hunt for specific information.

A third reason to do research is for yourself. Research is the perfect way to learn more about a hobby or interest. You might want to know more about hang gliding, action movies, or a favorite TV show. Hunting for information can be very exciting!

You can do research in many different places. Lots of people like to find information right at home. They use their own books or a computer with Internet access. The best place to do research, though, is at a library.[1]

Who knows your library inside and out? Your librarian.

Libraries in My Area

Make yourself a chart like the one below. It will help you keep track of libraries in your community.

	Library 1	Library 2
Name	Lincoln Public Library	Lincoln West Branch
Address	34 Broad Street	16 W. Ninth Street
Web address	www.write Web address here	www.write Web address here
Phone number	508-664-9300	508-664-9400
What days is it open?	Mon.–Sun.	Mon.–Sat.
What hours is it open?	10 a.m.–9 p.m.	10 a.m.–7 p.m.

Many people think of libraries as places to go to get books. But libraries are much more! Today's libraries are entire media centers. They have books, magazines, DVDs, CDs, and audio books. People go to libraries to use the Internet. Visitors also use the library's digital sources, such as databases with thousands of magazine articles. Libraries are a "one-stop shop."[2]

That's not all! Libraries have one great resource that you won't find anywhere else—the librarian, or media specialist.

Different Kinds of Libraries

Kids mostly use school and public libraries. If your town is large, it might have more than one public library. Many big cities have one main library, with smaller branch libraries in different parts of town. If you go to a branch library, you can request materials from all the other libraries in your town.

Colleges and universities also have libraries. You probably won't be able to check out materials, but you can usually go inside and use their resources.[3]

Another kind of library is the special collection. These libraries contain rare items that can't be found anywhere else. Special collections can include old books, maps, letters, legal documents, music, photographs, and pieces of art.

The Library of Congress is the most famous special collection in the United States. This library was founded in 1800. It has 134 million different items. It has more than 500 miles of bookshelves![4] The Library of Congress owns the first book printed in the United States. It also holds one of the first movies ever made, early baseball cards, and a photograph of Abraham Lincoln when he became president.

Librarians are specially trained to help people use the library. Think of librarians as detectives. They will hunt for information you need. They'll also help you learn to hunt for information on your own. You'll use this skill for your whole life.

People call the Library of Congress "America's attic." If you can't find a book here, you probably can't find it anywhere!

Take some time to get to know your library. You'll go back again and again.

2

What's at the Library, Anyway?

Before you start your research, get to know your library! You can start before you even go there. Most libraries have a Web site. If you have a computer at home, ask your parents to help you look for the site. You can also ask your school librarian or teacher to show you how.

If your public library has a Web site, you should see it right at the top of your results list. Click on the link and take a look. You'll see something like the site on the next page. You will find basic information, such as the library's address and phone number, when it's open, and how to get a library card. (Getting a library card is easy to do—after all, they really hope you'll come use the library!)

Many library Web sites let you search the library catalog. This is a huge database of all the items available in the library. A database is a large collection of information. Some Web sites even have a map or floor plan, so you can see how your library is organized.

Library Web sites also tell you about their services. The library might have computers for the public to use.

A Library Web Site

CENTRAL PUBLIC LIBRARY
THE WORLD OF KNOWLEDGE

MAIN PAGE   CALENDAR   PROGRAMS   JUST FOR KIDS   CONTACTS

WELCOME TO OUR LIBRARY

A Great Institution...
Since first opening its doors to the public in 1973, the Central Public Library has maintained its status of one of the City's most interesting places to gather, learn, connect, read and be transformed.
read more ▸▸

ABOUT THE LIBRARY

Frequently Asked Questions
How Do I Get A Library Card?
Become a library card-holder today »
How Do I Place a Hold on Library Materials?
Placing holds is easy, you can use the online catalog »
read more ▸▸

RECENT EVENTS

31, June 2007

Science Fair Research: Q & A
Event Type: Classes, Lectures & Workshops
Location: Goodson Regional

read more ▸▸

Subscribe news

e-mail   Enter
unsubscribe

PROGRAMS AND COURSES

Teen Volume Book Discussion Program ngaging book discussions for teens in high school, ages 14-19 throughout the city. The book *Sold* by Patricia McCormick will be discussed.
• Book Reviews by Kids Like You!   • Kids Vote! Elect to Read
• Teacher in the Library   • Teacher Resources
                                            • Parent Resources

Copyright © 2008 Central Public Library. All Rights Reserved

Terms of Use / Privacy Policy

New-York, USA
11 Some Street
New York, NY 02020

Tel/Fax: 1(800)123-4567
1(800)123-1234
E-mail: info@centralpubliclibrary.com

Taking a library tour will save you a lot of time. Your librarian can lead you to the right materials.

Many libraries also have programs and special events for kids. For example, a famous author might give a reading. Librarians often host a kids' book club. Some even show movies or have game nights.[5]

Once you get to the library, take a tour. You can look around by yourself, but the best way is to have a librarian give you a guided tour. Some libraries have helpful handouts and maps. Ask any librarian for help.

A tour might start at the library's circulation desk. This is where you go to check out books and other materials. Your next stop will probably be the library catalog. The catalog is almost always on a computer.

Most libraries have areas that are just for kids.

Most libraries have three main rooms or areas. One is especially for adults. The second is for children. The third area is the reference collection. The books in a reference collection are filled with easy-to-find facts. Encyclopedias and dictionaries are two types of reference books. Other kinds are atlases—books filled with maps—and town records. Library visitors use reference books so often that librarians want to keep them in the building. These books do not circulate. This means people cannot check them out and take them home. But you can read them right in the library, or you can photocopy the parts you need.[6]

Libraries keep fiction and nonfiction in separate sections. Fiction books are about made-up topics, and nonfiction books are about the real world. Fiction is usually arranged by authors' last names. Nonfiction books are what you mostly use for research. They are arranged by subject. For example, books about baseball are near other books about baseball—and also near books about

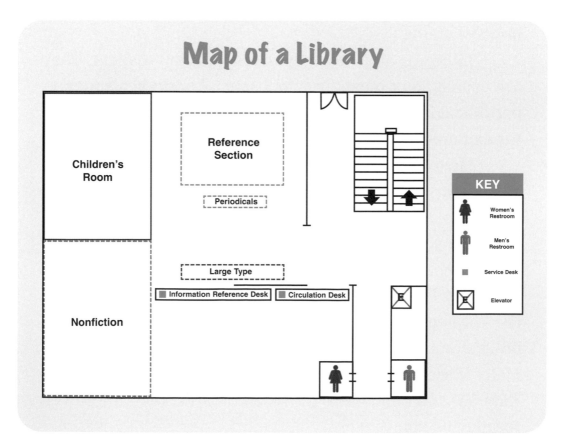

Map of a Library

Children's Room

Reference Section

Periodicals

Large Type

Information Reference Desk | Circulation Desk

Nonfiction

KEY

Women's Restroom

Men's Restroom

Service Desk

Elevator

other sports, like football and volleyball. Many libraries have a special nonfiction section for biographies—books about real-life people.

Librarians use a classification system to arrange books. The most popular system is called the Dewey decimal system. Every book gets its own call number. This is a series of numbers followed by letters or more numbers. The call number is printed on a sticker and taped on the spine of the book. On the shelf, books are arranged in order by call number. You can find out a book's call number in the library catalog.

Libraries also buy magazines and newspapers. They are usually kept on shelves in a special periodicals area. A periodical is a publication that comes out every so often— for example, once a week or once a month.

Most libraries have CDs, DVDs, and educational video games for visitors to check out. These materials have their own special areas, too.

On your tour, your librarian will show you where to find computers. Library computers have many different purposes. Some are just for librarians to use. Others hold the catalog or other databases about specific topics. On other computers, visitors can sign up to use the Internet. Many libraries have computers set up especially for kids. Kids use the computers for research and sometimes even for playing games.

Feldman/Owens · Animals Don't Wear Pajamas · Hen

Life Cycles

The Snake

Sat

Discovering Snakes and Lizards Nel

GAIL GIBBONS FROGS

PIGS WILL BE PIGS - AXELROD

rris

HORSES

SALAMANDERS

A Horse's Body

E AND WEXLER A Horse's Body

ick Hatches COLE AND WEXLER

call number

E 591. FEL

E 597 CRE

E 598.1 CUR

E 597. GIB

P AXE

E 636. MOR

E 591 BRO

E 597. BER

E 599. COL

E 598. COL

Each book on the shelf has a call number. You can see the call numbers at the bottom of this picture.

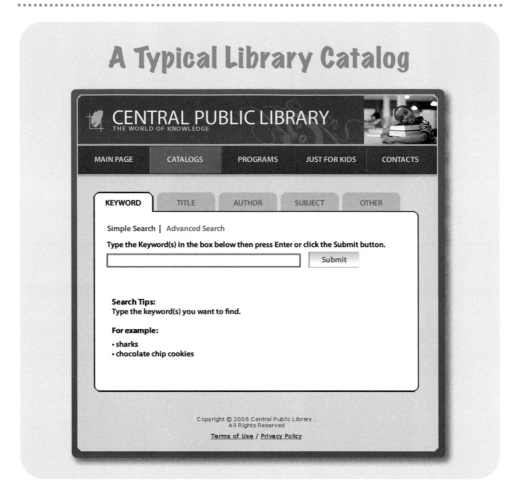

A Typical Library Catalog

CENTRAL PUBLIC LIBRARY
THE WORLD OF KNOWLEDGE

| MAIN PAGE | CATALOGS | PROGRAMS | JUST FOR KIDS | CONTACTS |

| KEYWORD | TITLE | AUTHOR | SUBJECT | OTHER |

Simple Search | Advanced Search

Type the Keyword(s) in the box below then press Enter or click the Submit button.

Submit

Search Tips:
Type the keyword(s) you want to find.

For example:
- sharks
- chocolate chip cookies

Copyright © 2008 Central Public Library .
All Rights Reserved
Terms of Use / Privacy Policy

Once you've looked around the library, you're ready to start your hunt for information. First, learn to use your library's catalog. Catalogs let you search in different ways. If you are looking for a specific book, you can do a title search. This means you type in the book's title. If you are looking for books by a certain author, you can do an author search. This means you type in the author's name.

You can also do a catalog search by subject or keyword. Let's say you want to learn about sharks. If you enter the word *shark* into the subject box and press ENTER, the screen will show a list of sources (see below). For each source, you'll see the title, author, and call number. Click on a source to see more information about it. Then you will find out when, where, and by what company the source was published.

Catalog Search Results for *Shark*

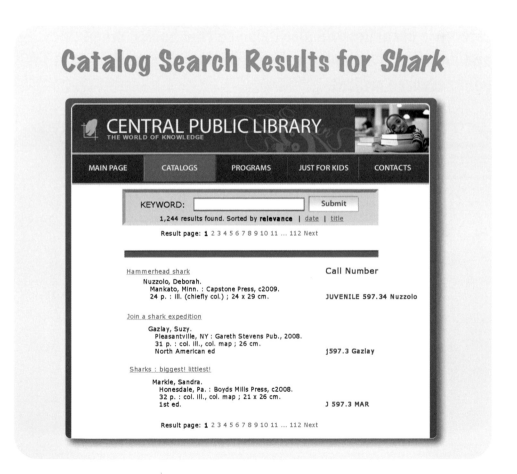

Reference Librarian: Your Neighborhood Detective

What's better than having a librarian at your library? Having two or three librarians! Big libraries have different kinds of librarians. The reference librarian's job is to help people do their research. This person sits at a special reference desk. He or she can show you how to use the library's reference materials. The reference librarian will also help you find books, magazines, and articles on a computer. You'll get lots of creative ideas for your research project.

Let's say you want to go and find a book on the shelf. First, write down the title and call number. (See the form below.) In the next chapter, you'll find out how to search for magazine and newspaper articles.

Books I Want to Find

Make yourself a form like the one below. It will help you keep track of the books you want to find on the shelves.

Type of source (check one):
- ☑ book
- ☐ audiobook
- ☐ DVD
- ☐ other

Name of author ____Briggs, Janet_____

Title ____Sharks Around the World_____

Call number ____598.4 BRI_____

Where is it? (check one)
- ☑ Nonfiction
- ☐ Fiction
- ☐ Children's section
- ☐ Magazine section
- ☐ Audio collection
- ☐ Reference
- ☐ Oversize

Before you even start your research, take some time to write a plan.

The Perfect Research Plan

So, your teacher has assigned you a research project. If you've already visited your library, you might want to rush there and begin your search. Slow down! Your project will turn out better if you create a plan for your assignment first. You'll save time and stay focused on your goals.

To make sure your paper will get finished in time, make a schedule. Figure out how long you have to do your assignment. Then give yourself due dates for each step. Experts say you should plan to spend about 35 percent of your time researching. You'll spend most of that time at the library. For the rest of your time, you will write and finish your project.[7]

Sharks are a popular topic for school reports. Use your library catalog to find the best sources.

When you start work on a school project, take some time to review your assignment. Even if you're doing research for fun, you should think about your goal. Write down what you already know about your topic. Next, make a list of the questions you want to answer.

Perhaps you're working on a poster about sharks. You want to know about their eating habits. Here are some examples of research questions: What do sharks eat? How much do they eat every day? How do they catch their food?

Now you can narrow your research topic even more. Perhaps you decide to find out how sharks use their sense of smell to find food.

After you come up with questions, it's time to brainstorm for keywords. These are the words you use to search in the library catalog. Keywords can be tricky, because you don't want them to be too general *or* too specific. For example, if you want to know about sharks, the keyword *fish* will give you too much information. A lot of sources about fish won't tell you anything about sharks! On the other hand, if you use the words *great white shark*, you'll only find information about one type of shark. That search is too narrow.

Your keywords should be somewhere in the middle. For a report about sharks, two good keywords might be *shark facts*. It also helps to write down synonyms for your keywords. That way you'll have lots of words to try. If the keywords *eating habits* don't help you, try using the synonym *diet*.

Now, think about the kind of information you are hoping to find. For a school assignment, you might have to include lots of facts. For a biography, you might need to find a person's diary or letters. Are you required to put quotations from experts in your research project? Make a checklist of requirements for your assignment, or use the rubric that your teacher gave you. A rubric is a list of

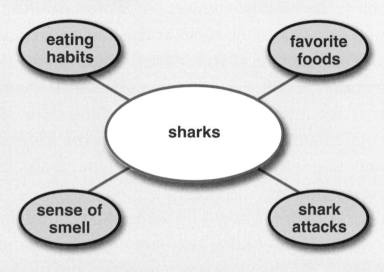

Spider Map

This is a spider map. The research topic is inside the center circle. In the outside circles, there are keywords to use in a hunt for information.

everything your teacher wants you to do for your research project. It's a road map to an A!

Your project might require you to use photographs or other illustrations. Pictures can show some things better than words can. For example, it's hard to describe the location of a shark's nostrils, but a picture or diagram does the job easily. You might also decide to look for maps, charts, or graphs. These visual elements make your project more complete and exciting for your audience.

Next, think about what kinds of sources you need. Books and magazines are great sources, but don't stop there. The Internet is a very popular source because it contains so much up-to-date information. You can find millions of pages full of information without ever leaving your chair! Just remember that not all information is *helpful* information. You'll find out how to tell the difference later in this book.

My Research Plan

What I want to find out: How sharks find food

My main question: How does a shark's sense of smell help it find food?

Other questions: What other animals have an excellent sense of smell? Do sharks see well? I remember hearing on TV that they can sense electricity. What does that mean?

Keywords I want to try: shark, food, prey, sense, smell, hunt, electricity

Sources I'd like to find: newspaper story about shark attack, DVD of sharks swimming underwater, book about sharks hunting, magazine article about sharks

Illustrations: diagram of shark jaw, map of hunting territory, chart of shark facts

Smart library users know which type of resource will help them most. Do you need a map, a photo, or a DVD?

Be "Information Smart"

The American Library Association (ALA) says that people in today's world must become "information smart." What does this mean? It's important for us all—students, teachers, parents, and others—to know "how to find, evaluate and use the best, most current information available to us." We need to know when to use books, when to search on a computer, and when to find another source. As the ALA says, we live in a world filled with information. The tricky part is finding the right information.[8]

Many organizations, such as the National Geographic Society and PBS, make excellent documentary movies about history or science. Your library probably has a wide selection of these educational films. Audio material, such as a recording of a scientist giving a talk, can be another great source.

Keep in mind that you can go beyond your own town's library. Let's say your library does not have a DVD about shark attacks. You can ask the librarian to borrow one through an interlibrary loan. That means your library will borrow the DVD from another library and then give the DVD to you.

Set yourself loose in the stacks. Find some helpful materials. It's time to dig in!

Working with Sources

Now that you have a plan, it's time to begin your research. If your teacher suggests it, start by finding basic information in a reference book, such as an encyclopedia. Then you can start your library catalog search. Maybe you already know about a great book on your topic. You have the name of the book or the author. Then you can do a title or author search. If you don't have a book in mind, start your catalog search with the keywords you have picked out.

When you get a results list, you will probably see that some titles will not help you. That might be because they are fiction books. Or perhaps they are about history, but you are only interested in information from this year. Pick out the sources that do look helpful. Write down their call numbers, and then find them on the shelves. If a promising source is already checked out, ask a librarian to put the title on hold. When the source gets returned, the library will give you a call.

Take your new sources to a table. Go through the books one by one. Your mission is to decide whether each book will help you answer your research questions. Use a book's table of contents to find out the titles of its chapters. Go to the very back of the book to find the index (see below). That's an alphabetical list of the subjects a

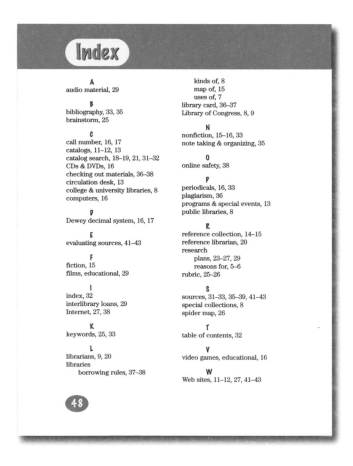

book talks about. Look for your research keywords in the index, and then turn to the pages listed. Quickly skim through the book. Look for good illustrations, charts, or maps.

If you decide a book will not be useful, put it aside right away. Don't waste your time! Look at the next one.

If you have found DVDs about your topic, look at their cases and read the descriptions. If you want to watch a movie, your library might have a place where you can view it there. Otherwise, you'll have to check it out to watch it at home.

The card catalog won't help you find some of the greatest sources—magazines and newspapers. Ask a librarian to show you how to use periodical indexes and databases. They will open up an entire new world of information.

You might find more sources than you can use right away. On the other hand, maybe you won't find enough. Maybe you used too many keywords, or your keywords were too specific. To find more sources, browse the library bookshelves. Go back to the area where you found one useful book, and look for others. You can also switch your keywords and do your search again. Now is the best time to get help from a librarian.

Here's another tip: Look inside your best sources to find more information. Did you know that nonfiction books usually have a bibliography at the end? A bibliography is a

What should you *do* with all those sources? Take notes!

list of all the sources that the author used to write the book. Use the bibliography like a miniature catalog. You might find some of these sources right in your own library!

What do you do once you've found good sources? Use them! As you read, take good notes. Notes will keep your facts straight as you create your paper, presentation, mural, or other project.

Note Organizer

This is an example of how to organize your notes as you do research.

My Research Topic: Sharks

My Question	The Answer	Where I Found It (Name of Source)
What are some names of different sharks?	great white, tiger, reef, nurse, hammerhead	Sharks by Felicia James, published by Wildlife Press, New York, 2008
What is the biggest type of shark?	whale shark	National Geographic News, http://write Web address here

Don't Steal People's Words!

Plagiarism is a serious mistake. When you plagiarize, you steal another person's work, such as words or pictures. Then you pretend the work is yours. You can avoid this by taking careful notes. Never write down exact sentences unless you are planning to use them as a quotation. When you do quote someone's words, make sure to place quotation marks (" ") around them. Be sure to tell your readers the name of the person who did the work you are using. Include the source in your bibliography.

Teachers think plagiarism is a very serious problem. If they think you plagiarized by mistake, they might let you rewrite the paper. If your teacher thinks you should have known the rules, you could be in big trouble.

You might want to take your best sources home. Then you can keep using them. First, you will have to get a library card. Your family might already have a card. If not, you will have to apply for one. The librarian will ask you to fill out a form with your name, address, and phone number. You might also have to pay a small fee. Then you will receive your library card.

To check out materials, go to the circulation desk. Hand the librarian the materials and your library card.

Library customers check out materials at the circulation desk.

Most libraries use a computer to scan your card and a label on the book. This records what you've checked out. Then the librarian will tell you when your materials are due. You will probably be able to keep books for about two weeks. Your library might have a limit on how many items you can check out. Then you'll have to make a few different trips.

Be sure to follow your library's borrowing rules. First, always return your materials on time. Other people are waiting to use your sources. Besides, if you don't meet your due date, you will have to pay a fine. If you need more time with a source, you can usually renew it. Another rule is to take good care of the materials you check out. Don't let anything become damaged! You will have to pay for a new copy.

Remember that some library sources cannot be checked out. If you need information from reference books or magazines, you have two choices. You can either take notes at the library or make a photocopy of the pages you need.

Online Safety

Everybody loves the Internet, right? It's a treasure chest of information. But it can also be a very dangerous place. Many Web sites are not appropriate for kids. Some Web sites ask people for personal information, such as their name, age, address, photograph, or telephone number.

To stay safe when you're on the Internet, get away from sites that make you feel uncomfortable. Never, ever give out personal information or send your photograph to a Web site without asking a trusted adult first. Most important, never make arrangements to go and see someone you have met on the Internet.[9]

My Shark Sources

1) <u>Sharks!</u> by John Stewart. Boston: Animals Press, 2006.

> nonfiction books

2) <u>Eating Like a Shark</u> by Sheila Ellsworth. New York: ABC Publishing, 2007.

3) "Shark Researchers Unite," <u>Springfield Gazette</u>, March 24, 2008, p. A5.

> newspaper article

3) <u>Sharks: Lions of the Sea</u>. Nature's Course, 2005.

> DVD

4) Amy O'Brien, "Shark Facts," <u>A to Z Sea Creatures</u>, 2008, http://www.write Web address here

> Web site

This girl is reading a reliable source. She can trust what it says. But remember: Not all sources are reliable!

If I Read It, It's True, Right?

Libraries are filled with interesting sources. How will you choose which ones to use for your research? You are going to evaluate them. This means you make sure that the sources have correct, helpful information. How can you do this?

First, check how old the source is. It's usually a good idea to look for up-to-date information. In the subject of science, for example, we discover new information every day. Even sources from three years ago might be wrong!

Next, check out the author. After you find a name, find out who the person is. In a good source, the author is an expert. For example, look for somebody who has studied sharks for many years.

If you're looking at a Web site, you want to know who created it. It could be an organization—like a college

41

Evaluating a Web Site

Use a checklist like this one to evaluate the Web sites you visit. It will help you decide whether the source is accurate and helpful.[10]

What is the address of the Web site? (The address usually starts with *http://www.*)

Check *Yes* or *No.*	Yes	No
Is the spelling correct?	☑	☐
Is the author's name and e-mail address on the page? (This could be a person or an organization.)	☑	☐
Are the links easy to find?	☑	☐
Are the words easy to read?	☐	☑
Is there a date that tells you when the page was made?	☑	☐
Do the photographs look real and professional?	☐	☑
Do the photographs on the site help you learn about the topic?	☑	☐
Does the site tell you who took the photographs?	☐	☑
Does the title tell you what the site is about?	☑	☐
Does the site answer some of your research questions?	☑	☐
Does the author of the page say things that you know are wrong?	☐	☑
Does the author include a bibliography (a list of the sources he or she used to make the Web site)?	☐	☑

or a museum—instead of a person. To find the author of a Web site, look at the bottom of the page. If you don't find any author information, ask a librarian or your teacher for help.

Also notice if the author mentions the sources that he or she used. You should stay away from books, articles, and Web sites that don't tell where they got their information. Always use sources that give you the chance to check what they say. Double-check some facts to see if they are accurate. On one site, you might see that a great white shark is 15 feet long. But a different site might say that the shark can be 40 feet long! Check a few more sources to make sure you get the real facts.

Last, make sure that the source is relevant to what you are writing. This means that it is closely related to your topic. An article on baby sharks might be interesting, but if you are researching the shark's sense of smell, it probably won't help you.

In time, you'll become comfortable using a library to do research. You'll be a pro on its wide variety of resources. You'll also learn how to work well with a librarian. Your library skills will help you all through school, in college, and as an adult.

Glossary

audio books—Books that are read aloud and recorded.

bibliography—A list of sources used to write a paper, article, or book.

brainstorm—To come up with ideas and write them down as they pop into your head.

call number—An assigned number that says where a library book should go on the shelves.

catalog—A computer database or collection of cards that lists all the sources that a library holds.

circulate—To move to and from a library, like a book when someone borrows and then returns it.

circulation desk—The desk where you check out library materials.

classification system—A system used to organize library materials, such as the Dewey decimal system.

databases—Collections of information kept on a computer.

Dewey decimal system—A system for organizing nonfiction books. Every book has a number that tells where it should go on a library shelf.

diagram—A plan or drawing that shows all the parts of something, such as a frog's body or a snowmobile.

documentaries—Nonfiction movies that present facts about a real person, place, or event.

evaluate—To decide if something is good or bad.

fiction—Writing that is based on imagination instead of fact.

illustrations—Drawn pictures in a book, article, or other source.

index—A list at the back of a book that tells you all the things you can read about in the book.

interlibrary loan—When libraries borrow materials from each other.

keyword—A word that a researcher uses to search for a topic in a catalog, database, or Internet search engine.

media—All the different forms that information can come in, including books, magazines, the Internet, radio programs, CDs, and DVDs.

nonfiction—A piece of writing about real people, places, and events.

plagiarism—Stealing someone else's work and pretending it is your own.

quotations—The exact words that a person spoke or wrote.

reference collection—A group of nonfiction materials including encyclopedias, atlases, and other sources of facts. These materials cannot be checked out of a library.

reference librarian—A librarian who helps people find information in reference sources.

relevant—Closely related to a certain topic.

renew—To extend the due date for a library item.

research—A hunt for information about a particular topic.

resource—A source of help or information.

rubric—A list of requirements for an assignment.

services—Ways to help customers or visitors. For example, a library provides the service of lending books.

skim—To look through a piece of writing quickly, without reading every word.

sources—Publications that supply information, such as books, articles, videos, and recordings.

spine—The part of a book that shows when a book is on a shelf.

synonyms—Words that have the same or a similar meaning as another word; for example, *large* and *big*.

Chapter Notes

1. Suzie Roth and Nick Corcodilos, "Library, not Internet, is best place to do research," *Emory-Riddle University Aeronautical Library Horizons*, January 26, 2007 <http://media.www.eraunews.com/media/storage/paper917/news/2007/01/26/News/Library.Not.Internet.Is.Best.Place.To.Do.Research-2678328.shtml> (August 27, 2008).

2. "A Library Advocate's Guide to Building Information Literate Communities," *American Library Association*, 2001 <http://www.ala.org/ala/advocacybucket/informationliteracy.pdf> (August 27, 2008).

3. "Visitor Information," *The Library, University of California Berkeley*, 2008 <http://www.lib.berkeley.edu/AboutLibrary/visitor_information.html> (August 27, 2008).

4. "Fascinating Facts About the Library," *Library of Congress*, May 1, 2008 <http://www.loc.gov/about/facts.html> (August 27, 2008).

5. "Game Night Begins at WBPL," *West Branch Public Library*, May 2007 <http://www.wbpl.org/archive/2007/05/game-night-news> (August 22, 2008).

6. "Reference Center," *Newark Public Library*, 2007 <http://www.npl.org/Pages/Collections/refdesk.html> (August 27, 2008).

7. Amy J. K. Borrell, "Write a Winning Research Report," *Scholastic Kids*, n.d. <http://content.scholastic.com/browse/article.jsp?id=1610> (February 17, 2008).

8. "A Library Advocate's Guide to Building Information Literate Communities," p. 3.

9. Larry Magrid, "Kids' Rules for Online Safety," *SafeKids.com*, 2004 and 2005 <http://www.safekids.com/kidsrules.htm> (August 29, 2008).

10. Kathleen Schrock, "Critical Evaluation of a Web Site, Elementary School Level," *Kathy Schrock's Guide for Educators*, 2006 <http://school.discoveryeducation.com/schrockguide/pdf/evalelem.pdf> (August 31, 2008).

Further Reading

Books

Bentley, Nancy. *Don't Be a Copycat! Write a Great Report Without Plagiarizing*. Berkeley Heights, N.J.: Enslow Publishers, 2008.

Hamilton, John. *Libraries and Reference Materials*. Edina, Minn.: ABDO Pub., 2005.

Terban, Marvin. *Ready! Set! Research! Your Fast and Fun Guide to Writing Research Papers That Rock* (Scholastic Guides). New York: Scholastic Reference, 2007.

On the Internet

Great Web Sites for Kids
http://www.ala.org/greatsites

Kentucky Virtual Library: All the Information in the Known Universe!
http://www.kyvl.org/kids/portal.html

Monroe County [Indiana] Public Library, How to Use the Dewey Decimal System
http://www.monroe.lib.in.us/childrens/ddchow.html

Index

WITHDRAWN